THE SHORTER ORKNEYINGA SAGA

THE HISTORY OF THE EARLS OF ORKNEY

Told by Tom Muir

&

Illustrated by Morag Ewing

Orkney Museums
and Heritage

ISBN: 0 9540320 7 1

Published by
Orkney Heritage

Designed and printed at
The Orcadian Limited
Hatston
Kirkwall
Orkney

This book is dedicated to
Sarah Traill Molony
&
Laura Ann Traill Molony

Although you live far away,
this is part of your heritage.

INTRODUCTION

The Orkneyinga Saga was written in Iceland around the year 1200. It was a story that had been told for many years, and the early part of it has more to do with legend than fact. The later part was nearer in time to the man who wrote it down for the first time, so it is likely to be more accurate. It tells the story of the Earls of Orkney, the powerful rulers who controlled these islands and who helped shape the destiny of Scandinavia during the Viking period and beyond. The last chapters were added later, around 1234-35, and the saga has been copied and changed several times since it was first written.

This version of the Orkneyinga Saga has been cut down so that the story is easier to follow than the original. It is a first step towards reading the full saga, and not intended to replace it. A lot of the original saga has been left out, but what are left are the main stories that make it so important to the history of Orkney. I have tried to keep the style of the original saga, with all its twists and turns. I hope that the reader enjoys this version, and one day reads the full Orkneyinga Saga, and some of the other wonderful sagas of the Icelanders.

Tom Muir,
February 2004.

SIGURD AND THE POISONED TOOTH

In the days when King Harald Fine-Hair ruled all of Norway, Vikings lived in Orkney and Shetland. Every summer they raided Norway with their longships, killing and stealing as they went. King Harald called all his warriors together and prepared a great fleet of longships. The king sailed west to Shetland, then south to Orkney where they killed the Vikings and captured the islands for King Harald. He carried on south to the Western Isles and as far as the Isle of Man, burning villages and killing as he went. Soon all the islands of Scotland belonged to King Harald Fine-Hair.

One of King Harald's most trusted friends was Rognvald, the Earl of More in Norway. His son Ivar had been killed in one of the battles, so King Harald gave Rognvald the gift of Orkney and Shetland in payment for the loss of his son. Earl Rognvald didn't want the islands, as they were too far away from his own lands in Norway. He asked his brother Sigurd if he would like the islands, and Sigurd said that he

ᛏᚼᛁ ᛊᛁᚼᚮᚱᛏᛁᚱ ᚮᚱᚲᛁ�101ᛁᚾᚷᛁ ᛊᚪᚷᚪ

would. King Harald gave Sigurd the title of Earl of Orkney and Shetland, and Sigurd remained behind to rule the islands. Sigurd the Powerful, as he was called, became a mighty leader. After a while he thought that Orkney and Shetland were not big enough for him, and he led his warriors south into Scotland. He won many battles, and was soon the ruler of much of the North of Scotland.

There was a Scottish earl called Maelbrigte Tusk who refused to have his land taken from him by this army of Vikings. People called him Tusk because he had a large tooth that stuck out of his mouth. He sent messengers to Sigurd and arranged to have a meeting to try to make peace. They agreed to take forty men each to the meeting. Sigurd didn't trust the Scottish earl, and he told his men to take forty horses but for two men to sit on each horse. When the riders got closer Tusk saw that there were two sets of legs on either side of the horses, and he knew that he had been tricked. He ordered his men to get ready to fight, saying that they should try to kill at least one man before they died. When Sigurd saw that the Scots would fight he ordered his men to prepare for battle. The extra warriors got off their horses and crept around to the back of the Scots. The warriors on horseback rode at the Scottish men, swords slashing down on them. The Scots started to fall back, and then Sigurd's other men who were on foot attacked from behind. The Scots were surrounded, and after a hard fought battle Tusk and all of his men were killed.

ᛏᚼᛁ ᛊᚼᛟᚱᛏᛖᚱ ᛟᚱᚲᚾᛈᚨᛁᚾᚷᚨ ᛊᚨᚷᚨ

Sigurd was happy with his victory, and he decided to make a show of his success in battle. He ordered his men to cut off the heads of the dead Scots and to tie them to their saddles as a warning to others. Sigurd cut Tusk's head off and tied it to his own saddle. As he spurred his horse to gallop off, the head swung against his leg and the tooth that stuck out of Tusk's mouth scratched him. After a while the scratch became painful and it swelled up. Blood poisoning had set in, and this led to the death of Sigurd the Powerful. Maelbrigte Tusk had got his revenge on his killer. They buried Sigurd by the banks of the River Oykel on the Dornoch Firth, and raised a great mound over his grave.

ᚦᚢᛖ ᛊᚺᚩᚱᛏᛖᚱ ᚩᚱᚲᚤᛗᚨᛁᚾᚷᚨ ᛊᚨᚷᚨ

THE KILLING OF HALFDAN HIGH-LEG

Sigurd the Powerful's son Guthorm ruled for a year, but he died childless. The earldom of Orkney was given to Earl Rognvald's son Hallad, but he was a weak leader and soon the Vikings drove him out of Orkney and he returned to Norway in shame. Two Danish Vikings called Thorir Tree-Beard and Kalf Scurvy took over the islands and used them as a base to raid from. Earl Rognvald was furious, and called his sons to him. His eldest son Hrolf was away raiding at the time. He would become the first ruler of Normandy. Thorir offered to go, but his father said that his future was to succeed him as the Earl of More. Hrollaug offered to go, but Rognvald refused, saying that his future lay in Iceland. Earl Rognvald's youngest son was called Einar, but his father hated him and wanted nothing to do with him. His mother was a slave woman; he was tall and ugly and had only one eye. He asked Rognvald for the earldom, with the promise that if he went to Orkney then his father would never have to see him again. Rognvald liked this idea, and gave him the earldom of Orkney and Shetland. Einar sailed to Orkney and killed the Viking leaders. He soon took control of the whole of the islands and was given the nickname Turf Einar, because it was said that he was the first to cut peats for fuel in Orkney.

King Harald Fine-Hair had two sons called Halfdan High-Leg and Gudrod Gleam. They grew up to be violent men, killing the king's earls and taking their land. They rode to More where they attacked Earl Rognvald and killed him. King Harald went into a rage when he heard the news, and he set out after his sons. Gudrod surrendered and begged his father to forgive him. Halfdan High-Leg sailed west to Orkney and drove Turf Einar out of the islands. Einar gathered warriors and sailed back to Orkney. Halfdan sailed out to do battle off North Ronaldsay, and their ships were tied together so that the battle could be fought with swords and spears. Einar's men were winning the battle, and most of Halfdan's men lay dead or wounded in the bottom of the ships. Halfdan could see that he had lost the fight, so he jumped overboard and swam to the nearby shore. The next morning Einar saw what looked like a man moving around on the island. He went ashore and found Halfdan High-Leg and killed him. He made poems about how he had avenged his father's death, and he shamed his brothers for doing nothing.

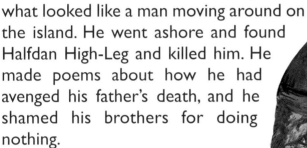

When King Harald heard that his son had been killed by Turf Einar he gathered a fleet and sailed to

ᛏᚺᛁ ᛖᚺᛟᚱᛏᛁᚱ ᛟᚱᚲᚺᚣᛅᛁᚾᚷᚨ ᛋᚨᚷᚨ

Orkney. Einar escaped to Caithness where he hid from the king. He sent messengers to King Harald and asked for peace talks.

King Harald agreed, and claimed a fine of sixty gold marks from the islands for the killing of his son. Einar offered to pay all of the fine himself, as long as everyone gave their land to him and paid him rent. Turf Einar lived for many years after that, and died in his bed.

ᛏᚺᛉ ᛋᚺᛟᚱᛏᛉᚱ ᛟᚱᚲᚾᛦᚨᛁᚾᚷᚨ ᛋᚨᚷᚨ

THE MAGIC BANNER

Earl Turf Einar had three sons called Arnkel, Erlend and Thorfinn Skull-Splitter. They ruled Orkney after their father's death. Arnkel and Erlend died in battle fighting for King Eirik Blood-Axe, who was another son of King Harald Fine-Hair. Thorfinn Skull-Splitter's son Hlodvir became Earl of Orkney, and married Eithne, the daughter of King Kjarval of Ireland. They had a son called Sigurd the Stout, who became Earl of Orkney after his father died.

Sigurd the Stout was a great warrior, and he defended the lands in Caithness that had been won in battle. A Scottish earl called Finnleik challenged him to a battle in Caithness. Sigurd knew that he would be outnumbered seven to one, and that there was no way that he could win. He went to see his mother, who was known to be a very powerful witch. He told her about the battle, and asked her for help. The old woman gave Sigurd a hard look, and said that if she thought that he would live forever then she would have reared him in her wool basket. She took a roll of cloth and handed it to Sigurd. She told him it was a banner that was woven using all the magic that she knew, and that the banner would bring victory to the side that carried it, but it would bring death to the man who held it. Sigurd took the banner and left.

ᛏᚺᛁ ᛋᚺᛢᚱᛏᛗᚱ ᛢᚱᚲᛗᛗᛁᚾᚷᚠ ᛋᚠ�

The magic banner had been made by Eithne, who muttered spells over it as she worked. It was embroidered with the figure of a flying raven. When it flew from its pole the raven seemed to be flying in front of the army. Sigurd the Stout met the Scottish earl at Skitten in Caithness, and the banner was flown for the first time. He had promised the people of Orkney that he would give them back the rights to their land that Turf Einar had taken from them if they would help him fight this battle. When the two sides clashed, the standard-bearer who held the banner was killed. Another man was ordered to carry it, but he too was cut down in the battle. A third standard-bearer took the banner, and he too was killed. By this time Sigurd's army had won the battle, with the help of the magic raven banner.

In 995 King Olaf Tryggvason arrived in Orkney and captured Earl Sigurd at Osmundwall, Hoy, where he had three ships ready to go on a raid. Olaf was sailing to Norway with five longships to claim the throne. He forced Sigurd and all his men to renounce the old gods and to convert to Christianity. If they didn't, King Olaf threatened to have them all killed and to go through the islands, burning and slaughtering as he went. Olaf took Sigurd's son Hundi as a hostage, and sailed to Norway. Hundi did not live long, and after his death Sigurd returned to the worship of Odin and Thor.

Sigurd the Stout was killed at the Battle of Clontarf in Ireland on Good Friday 1014.* He was supporting King Sigtrygg Silk-Beard who was fighting against the Christian King Brian. Sigurd took his magic raven banner with him and had it flown at the head of his army. The battle was a long and hard one with many men killed on both sides. Sigurd's men were in the centre of the battle line, and soon the

standard-bearer who carried the raven banner was killed. Sigurd ordered another man to carry it, and this man too was killed. Sigurd ordered Thorstein Hallsson to pick it up, but Amundi the White warned him that every man who held the banner would die. Sigurd then ordered Raven the Red to carry the banner, but he refused, saying 'Carry your fiend yourself!' Sigurd tore the magic raven banner from the pole, and tucked it into his clothes. Soon after, Sigurd the Stout was pierced through by a spear and died. King Brian was also killed in the battle, but his army won the day. Sigtrygg Silk-Beard ran away from the battlefield, followed by what was left of his army.

Back in Orkney the people had not heard that Sigurd had been killed in battle. A man called Harek saw the ghosts of Earl Sigurd and some of his men returning home, and he took a horse and rode out to meet them. People saw them meet, and then they went behind a hill and disappeared from sight. Harek and Sigurd the Stout's ghostly army were never seen again.

* The story of the Battle of Clontarf is not given in any detail in the Orkneyinga Saga, but this account comes from the Icelandic 'Njal Saga.'

ᛏᚼᛁ ᛊᚼᚭᚱᛏᚢᚱ ᚭᚱᚲᚼᚤᚨᛁᚾᚷᚨ ᛊᚨᚷᚨ

DEATH AT THE FEAST

Sigurd the Stout had four sons. Sumarlidi, Brusi and Einar Wry-Mouth by his first wife, and Thorfinn, whose mother was the daughter of King Malcolm of Scotland. Thorfinn was raised at the court of the Scottish King, who gave him the Scottish earldoms of Caithness and Sutherland. He grew up to be a tall but ugly man with black hair, sharp features, a big nose and bushy eyebrows. He was also very greedy and ruthless. When Thorfinn's half-brother Sumarlidi died he demanded a third share of Orkney. Brusi would have agreed, but Einar Wry-Mouth refused, and took two thirds of the islands for himself. He was a cruel and hard man, and he raised the taxes in Orkney to pay for his Viking raids. One man called Thorkel who lived in Deerness spoke out against the taxes, and was forced to flee for his life. He went to Caithness and became Thorfinn's foster-father. He became known as Thorkel the Fosterer.

When Thorfinn came of age he repeated his demands for a third of Orkney. Einar once more refused, and both men gathered an army to do battle. Brusi went between his two brothers and managed to make peace. It was agreed

ᛏᚺᛁ ᛋᚺᛟᚱᛏᛁᚱ ᛟᚱᚲᚾᛁᚨᛁᚾᚷᛁ ᛋᚨᚷᚨ

that Thorfinn should share a third of the islands. When Thorkel the Fosterer went to Orkney to gather taxes he discovered that Einar Wry-Mouth was plotting to kill him. He sailed to Norway, where he was joined by Thorfinn. When they arrived back in Orkney Einar raised an army to attack them. Brusi again made peace, and it was arranged that Einar and Thorkel should put aside their old hatred of each other, and that both men should hold a feast for each other. Earl Einar was to go to Deerness for a feast at Thorkel's hall, and then Thorkel was to go to Earl Einar's hall for another feast.

Einar Wry-Mouth arrived at Thorkel's hall, and the best food and drink was brought to him. He was in a very bad mood, and there was little sign of friendship between the two men. When the feast was over Thorkel was to ride to Earl Einar's hall, but he did not trust the earl. He sent spies to check out the road that he had to travel. They returned and told him that there were armed men waiting in ambush for him at three different parts of the road. Earl Einar was in an even worse mood by this time, as Thorkel was late in leaving. When Thorkel walked into the room Einar said to him, 'Aren't you ready yet?' 'Yes, I'm ready now' said Thorkel, and he drew his sword and brought it down with all of his might on Einar's head. Earl Einar fell dead into the fire. An Icelander who was with Thorkel said 'I've never seen such a useless lot, can't you

ᛏᚺᛇ ᛊᚺᛟᚱᛏᛖᚱ ᛟᚱᚲᚺᚤᛆᛁᚾᚷᚨ ᛊᚨᚷᚨ

pull the earl out of the fire?' and with that he hooked his curved axe around Einar's neck and pulled his body up onto one of the benches. Thorkel ran outside where his men were waiting with drawn swords. Earl Einar's men were outnumbered, and so they took the body of their leader home.

ᛏᚼᛉ ᛊᚼᛟᚱᛏᛉᚱ ᛟᚱᚲᚼᚢᚨᛁᚼᚷᚨ ᛊᚨᚷᚨ

THE SEA BATTLE

Earl Thorfinn tried to get control of his half-brother Einar's third share of Orkney, but Earl Brusi refused. Brusi sailed to Norway to get the support of King Olaf for his claim. Olaf decided to claim the one third of Orkney for himself, but he put Brusi in charge of it. Thorfinn kept his third share. Brusi's young son Rognvald was left behind in Norway and was fostered by King Olaf.

King Olaf was killed at the Battle of Stikelstad in 1030, and was afterwards made a saint. Rognvald was also at the battle, although he was only a youth at the time. He saved Olaf's brother, Harald, who had been badly wounded. This man was later King Harald the Hard-Ruler. Rognvald escaped to Russia where he lived for several years. When he returned to Norway he learnt that his father had died, and he asked King Magnus, his foster-brother, for his share of Orkney. He was given his father's third, along with the king's third. Rognvald sent messengers to Orkney, but they were not made welcome by Earl Thorfinn who had been ruling all of Orkney alone. Thorfinn was now very powerful, as he had invaded and taken by force the Western Isles, much of Scotland and part of Ireland. He was now called Thorfinn the Mighty, but he was having trouble with enemies who were raiding his lands. He agreed to share Orkney with Rognvald, and said that he

ᛏᚺᛖ ᛊᚺᚨᚱᛏᛖᚱ ᛟᚱᚲᚾᚤᛁᛜᚨ ᛊᚨᚷᚨ

could keep the king's third of the islands as well as his own, but not to speak about it again.

Rognvald and his uncle Thorfinn ruled over Orkney in peace for several years. Thorfinn lived in Caithness for most of the time while Rognvald lived in Orkney. Earl Rognvald built a church that was dedicated to his foster-father St. Olaf in the small trading village of Kirkwall. Things went well until a troublemaker called Kalf Arnason was driven from Norway with a large band of warriors. They lived with Thorfinn in Caithness, as Thorfinn was married to Kalf's niece, Ingibjorg. Kalf started to stir up trouble between Thorfinn and Rognvald by saying that Thorfinn should have the king's third of Orkney, as he had so many warriors to feed. Thorfinn sent messengers to Rognvald demanding more land in Orkney. Rognvald refused, and both sides gathered together warriors for a battle. Rognvald was given warriors and longships by his foster-brother King Magnus, who also sent a message to Kalf Arnason that his lands in Norway would be returned if he fought for Rognvald.

Earl Rognvald sailed to Caithness with thirty ships to do battle with Earl Thorfinn the Mighty. On their way south they met Thorfinn with a fleet of sixty ships. Although Thorfinn had more ships, Rognvald's ships were much larger. The ships were tied together with grappling hooks, and the battle started. The fighting was fierce, with many warriors killed on both sides. Thorfinn's smaller ships were being swept clean by Rognvald's warriors, and Thorfinn saw that he was losing the fight. Kalf Arnason had arrived with six large ships, but didn't take part in the battle.

ᛏᚺᛁ ᛊᚺᛟᚱᛏᛁᚱ ᛟᚱᚲᚺᛘᛅᛁᚺᚷᚨ ᛊᚨᚷᚨ

Thorfinn cut the grappling ropes and sailed to Kalf. He pleaded with him to help, saying that if he died then Kalf would have no friends and nowhere to run. Kalf ordered his ships to attack the smaller ships in Rognvald's fleet, and soon killed the warriors in them as his ships were much higher. When the Norwegian warriors saw this they fled, leaving Rognvald to fight alone. Thorfinn and Kalf attacked Rognvald's ship, killing many of his men. Seeing that the battle was lost, Rognvald cut the grappling ropes and sailed away. He headed straight for the open sea and sailed to Norway.

ᛏᚻᛖ ᛊᛖᚨᛒᛏᛚᛖ ᛟᚱᚲᚺᛗᚨᛁᚾᚷᚨ ᛊᚨᚷᚨ

THE BURNING OF THE EARLS

After the sea battle, Thorfinn swept through Orkney, killing Earl Rognvald's supporters and making everyone swear an oath of loyalty to him. Thorfinn now lived in Orkney, and sent Kalf Arnason to the Western Isles to rule there in his place. Rognvald lived in Norway with his foster-brother, King Magnus.

After a while Rognvald went to King Magnus and said that he wanted to try to get his earldom back from Thorfinn. King Magnus offered Rognvald ships and men to lead an invasion, but Rognvald refused, saying that Thorfinn's army was too powerful to fight in a battle. Instead he asked for one longship with a hand picked crew. King Magnus agreed, and Rognvald sailed west to Orkney. He landed in the Mainland and soon found out where Thorfinn was staying. That night Rognvald and his men prepared to attack Thorfinn when he wasn't expecting it. It was late, and most of the men in Thorfinn's house were asleep, but Thorfinn was still sitting drinking. Rognvald's men blocked up all of the doors, then set fire to the farmhouse. The first that Thorfinn knew was when the house was ablaze. He sent a messenger to the door to ask who had done this. The messenger was told that it was Earl Rognvald.

ᛏᚺᛁ ᛋᚺᛟᚱᛏᛁᚱ ᛟᚱᚲᚾᚤᛁᚾᚷᛅ ᛋᛅᚷᛅ

He then asked if they could go outside, and it was agreed to let the women and slaves out, but Rognvald said it would be better if Thorfinn and his men were dead. A door was cleared and the terrified women and slaves were let out of the burning building.

By now the house was burning fiercely, and thick smoke filled the rooms. Thorfinn kicked out one of the wooden panels that made up the walls of his house, and with his wife Ingibjorg in his arms, he jumped through the hole and escaped under the cover of the smoke and darkness. Nobody saw him escape. He took a small boat and rowed all the way to Caithness where he hid with friends. Rognvald thought Thorfinn was dead, and he sent messengers to Caithness and the Western Isles to proclaim himself their ruler.

Just before Christmas Rognvald sailed to Papa Stronsay to collect malt for making his Yule beer. That night on the island they were all sitting by the fire when the man who was tending it said that they were running out of firewood. Rognvald said that they would be old enough when the fire had burnt out. He realized that he had made a slip of the tongue, as he had meant to say 'warm enough.' This he took to be a bad sign, as his foster-father King Olaf had made a slip of the tongue before he was killed in battle, and he had told Rognvald that if he should do the same then he wouldn't have long to live. 'Perhaps my uncle Thorfinn is alive after all,' said Rognvald. No sooner had he said this than a great noise was heard outside. Thorfinn and his men had set the house on fire. It was agreed that all but Rognvald and his men should be let out, and a door was opened. The people who left had to be helped over a pile of brushwood that was set in front of the door. One man in a night shirt came to the door and was offered a hand, as the men thought he was a deacon. The man put his hand on the brushwood and vaulted over the heads of Thorfinn's men. It was known that only Earl Rognvald could do such a feat. A search was made and Rognvald was discovered hiding on the shore. He was discovered because he had taken his lapdog with him, and it was heard barking among the rocks. Thorkel the Fosterer found Rognvald and killed him. Thorfinn killed all of Rognvald's men, but sent one of his supporters to Norway to tell the king.

THE FORTUNE TELLER

King Magnus died, leaving his uncle Harald the Hard-Ruler as king of all of Norway. Earl Thorfinn made friends with King Harald, and later went on a pilgrimage to Rome. He built a fine church in Birsay dedicated to Christ and brought the first bishop to Orkney. Thorfinn the Mighty died an old man and was buried in the fine church in Birsay that he had built.

Thorfinn had two sons, Paul and Erlend. They did not divide Orkney, but ruled it together peacefully. In 1066 King Harald the Hard-Ruler arrived in Orkney with a large fleet of ships. He was on his way to invade England, as he had a claim to the throne. The two Earls of Orkney raised an army and joined him on the expedition. King Harald left his wife and two daughters behind in Orkney and sailed south. They landed in the north of England and captured a place called Stamford Bridge. King Harald the Hard-Ruler left his ships and headed inland with some of his army, but was attacked and killed by King Harold Godwinsson of England. King Harald's son Olaf, and the Earls of Orkney had been left on the ships, but they rushed to attacked King Harold Godwinsson and his army. They lost the battle, but were allowed to sail away after the fighting was over. It was said that King Harald's daughter Maria died in Orkney at the very same moment that her father was killed. It was said that they shared only one life between them.

Earl Paul had a son called Hakon and Earl Erlend had two sons called Erling and Magnus. Hakon and Erling were hot headed and violent, while Magnus was good and kind. Hakon hated his cousins, and thought he was more important than they were. It got so bad that the two earls fell out over their sons fighting. It was suggested that Hakon should be sent away, for the sake of peace. He went to Norway, then to Sweden. When he was in Sweden he heard of a wizard who could tell a man's fortune, and he set off to look for him. Hakon asked the old man if he would one day rule all of Orkney by himself. The wizard told him to come back in three days and he would have his answer. When Hakon returned the old man told him that he would indeed rule all of Orkney, but his journey back there would bring dangerous times. He also said that in his life he would commit a great crime, one that he may never be forgiven for. Hakon was happy; he had got the answer he wanted.

ᛏᚻᛁ ᛋᚻᚯᚱᛏᛖᚱ ᚯᚱᚲᚻᚤᛅᛁᚾᚷᛖ ᛋᚨᚷᚨ

THE BATTLE OF THE MENAI STRAIT

King Magnus Barelegs was now on the throne of Norway. Hakon had heard that he was not wanted back in Orkney and that his father held little power there. Hakon knew that the king was a greedy man, and he urged him to launch an invasion fleet west to conquer the islands like King Harald Fine-Hair had done. King Magnus said that if he did that then all the islands could expect to be treated harshly. Hakon didn't like the sound of that and kept quiet. It was too late; King Magnus was now making plans to attack.

A large fleet of longships sailed west from Norway, bringing with it a huge army. In Orkney King Magnus captured the Earls Paul and Erlend, and had them sent into exile in Norway, where they both died. Instead of Hakon being made Earl of Orkney as he had hoped, King Magnus Barelegs put his eight year old son Sigurd in charge of the islands. He then took Earl Erlend's sons Erling and Magnus with him and sailed south. King Magnus swept through the Western Isles with fire and swords, and continued south as far as Wales. Here King Magnus was faced with an army led by two earls, Hugh the Stout and Hugh the Proud. Their ships landed at the Menai Strait and all the warriors prepared for battle. All except Magnus Erlendsson from Orkney. He refused to fight, saying that he had no quarrel with anyone there. Instead he picked up his psalm book and started to sing psalms. The battle raged around him, first with arrows then with hand to hand fighting. Hugh the Proud put up a fierce fight, and was so completely covered with armour that only his eyes were showing. King Magnus told an archer that they should both aim for his eyes. They both fired their arrows, one struck Hugh on the nose-guard of his helmet but the other went straight through his eye, killing him instantly. It was said that the king's arrow found its mark.

King Magnus had made Magnus Erlendsson his cup bearer, but he was furious with him for refusing to fight. One night when the ships were close to the Scottish shore Magnus made up his bed to look as if someone was sleeping in it. Dressed only in his underwear he swam ashore and then ran into the woods to hide. When King Magnus discovered that he had gone he set his bloodhounds after him. One of the dogs found the tree that Magnus was hiding in, but he threw a stick at it which hit the dog on the leg and sent it off back to the ships with its tail between its legs. The other dogs followed it, and Magnus was saved. He travelled to the court of the Scottish king, and then south to England. He never returned to Orkney while King Magnus Barelegs was alive.

ᛏᚺᛁ ᛊᚺᛟᚱᛏᛖᚱ ᛟᚱᚲᚴᛁᛁᛝᚷᚨ ᛊᚨᚷᚨ

THE MURDER OF ST MAGNUS

After the death of King Magnus, Hakon became Earl of Orkney. Magnus Erlendsson returned to Orkney to claim his half of the earldom, but Hakon refused. Both men raised an army to fight for the islands, but peacemakers were able to settle the dispute and it was agreed that they would share the islands between them. Each earl had a half share, and they defended the islands together. They were now friends, but this was not to last.

Troublemakers stirred up hatred in Earl Hakon's heart, as Hakon was jealous of Earl Magnus because he was very popular and well liked by the people of Orkney. It got so bad that the two men raised armies and attacked each other's property. A peace meeting was arranged on the Mainland, and oaths were sworn and the two earls shook hands. Earl Hakon suggested another peace meeting during Easter, to be held on the island of Egilsay. Magnus did not suspect that he was in any danger, and he agreed to the meeting. Both earls were to have just two ships and a certain number of men. Magnus picked his wisest and his most peace-loving followers to go to Egilsay with him.

On the day arranged, Magnus set out for Egilsay with his

two ships. It was a beautiful calm day and the ships had to be rowed as there was no wind. Suddenly a large breaker rose out of the calm sea and towered high over the ship that Magnus was steering. It crashed down on the spot where Magnus was sitting, soaking him to the bone. The men thought it was a bad omen, but Magnus refused to turn back. When they arrived on Egilsay they saw that Hakon was approaching with eight ships, not two as had been agreed. They knew that they had been tricked, and that their lives were in danger. Magnus went to the church that was there and spent the night in prayer.

The next day Magnus gave himself up to Hakon and his warriors. They said that there was to be no more joint rule in Orkney, and that it was going to be decided that very day. Knowing that Hakon meant to kill him, Magnus gave him three choices. It was not out of fear of death, but to save Hakon's soul from being condemned to Hell. His first offer was that he would go on a pilgrimage to the Holy Land with two ships

ᛏᚺᛁ ᛋᚺᚬᚱᛏᛁᚱ ᚬᚱᚲᚺᛘᚨᛁᛏᚷᚨ ᛋᚨᚷᚨ

and swear that he would never return. This offer was rejected. His second offer was that he would go to Scotland to Hakon's friends and be kept locked up. This second offer was also turned down. Magnus's third offer was to be mutilated or blinded and cast into a dungeon. Hakon accepted this offer, but his leading chieftains said that they would no longer serve two earls, and that one of them must die. Hakon pointed to Magnus and said 'Better kill him then,' and so it was decided.

Earl Hakon's standard bearer Ofeig was told to do the killing, but he refused. Hakon then ordered the cook Lifolf to kill Magnus, and he was forced to obey. Magnus forgave Lifolf, as he was doing this deed against his will. He prayed for forgiveness and placed his soul in God's hands. Magnus told Lifolf to stand in front of him and strike him a hard blow on the head, as it was not fitting for a chieftain to be beheaded like a thief. Lifolf swung the axe, and Magnus's soul passed to Heaven.

ᛏᚻᛂ ᛋᚻᚩᚱᛏᛂᚱ ᚩᚱᚲᚻᛉᚪᛁᚾᚷᚪ ᛋᚪᚷᚪ

MIRACLES

Magnus had died on the 16th April about the year 1116. His body lay where it had fallen, as Earl Hakon refused to allow Magnus's supporters to bury it. Hakon and his men then went to Paplay in Holm where Magnus's mother Thora was to hold a feast to celebrate the peace treaty. When Hakon arrived alone Thora guessed that her son had been killed. She served Earl Hakon at the table herself. When many hours had passed she spoke quietly to Hakon, begging him to allow her to bury her son. The tears that rolled down her cheeks made Hakon ashamed of his crime, and he told her to bury her son where she liked.

Magnus' body was carried to the Mainland, where it was buried in Christ Church in Birsay. The spot where Magnus had died was a rocky place where only moss grew. After his death it was turned into a green field. Strange lights were seen to float around his tomb, and the air was filled with the sweet smell of perfume. People started to pray to Magnus when they were ill, and they were soon cured. People started to say that Magnus was a saint, but they had to be careful as Earl Hakon would have become angry with them. Bishop William supported Earl Hakon and did not believe that Magnus was a saint. Hakon ruled Orkney alone for many years. He went on a pilgrimage to the

ᛏᚺᛁ ᛋᚺᛟᚱᛗᚱ ᛟᚱᚲᚺᚢᛁᚾᚷᛁ ᛋᚨᚷᚨ

Holy Land to try to find forgiveness for the sin of killing Magnus. He ruled Orkney for many years after the killing of Magnus and became a popular earl. Hakon died in his bed, and was greatly missed by the people of Orkney. He left two sons by different mothers. Harald Smooth-Tongue was the son of Helga, the daughter of a rich farmer from Caithness. His other son was called Paul the Silent. These two half-brothers hated each other, and people could see that there would be trouble ahead.

ᛏᚼᛁ ᛊᚼᛟᚱᛏᛁᚱ ᛟᚱᚲᚾᛁᚨᛁᚾᚷᚨ ᛊᚨᚷᚨ

THE POISONED SHIRT

Earl Paul the Silent lived in Orkney and was popular with the people. His half-brother, Harald Smooth-Tongue, lived in Caithness, which had been given to him by the King of Scots. Harald was not well liked, and it was said that he did what his mother and her evil sister Frakokk told him to do. Harald and his family and friends moved to Orkney and lived at the Bu in Orphir. There had been trouble between the two earls, and a peace meeting was called. It was agreed that they should spend more time together, especially during festivals like Christmas.

Harald Smooth-Tongue decided to hold a great Christmas feast at his hall in Orphir, and Paul the Silent and his followers were invited. There was a lot of work to be done to prepare all of the food that would be needed, and everyone was busy. Harald's mother, who was called Helga, and her sister Frakokk were busy too. They were making a shirt of milk-white linen, embroidered with gold thread that made it sparkle like sunshine on snow. Harald Smooth-Tongue came into their room and saw the beautiful shirt. He asked them who this shirt was for, and they said that it was for his half-brother Paul. Harald was very angry, and said that they didn't take so much care in

making fine clothes for him. He picked it up and looked at it; it was so lovely that he wanted it. His mother tried to snatch it away from him, saying he had no need to be jealous of his brother's clothes. Harald was just about to put the shirt on when his mother and her sister started to cry, they tore off their bonnets and pulled their hair, saying that his life was at risk if he put on the shirt. Harald ignored them and put on the beautiful snow-white shirt. No sooner was the shirt on his back when he was gripped by a sudden, burning pain. He screamed out in agony, his body shook and his flesh felt as if it was on fire. He was put to his bed, but died after a short time. The shirt that was made for his half-brother was poisoned, and when Paul heard about it he sent Helga and Frakokk away from Orkney. They lived in Caithness, then later in Sutherland where Frakokk had land. The evil Frakokk raised Harald's young son Erlend, along with her grandsons Olvir Brawl and Thorbjorn Clerk. Those boys would grow up to be warriors who would later bring trouble to Orkney and its earls.

MAGNUS IS MADE A SAINT

After the death of Harald Smooth-Tongue his half-brother, Paul the Silent, ruled all of Orkney by himself. During this time people continued to visit the tomb of Earl Magnus, praying for cures from illness and blindness. More and more people were cured, but still Bishop William refused to believe them. On a trip back from Norway Bishop William was caught in a storm and was forced to stay in Shetland. The weather continued to be bad, and it looked like the bishop would have to stay there for the rest of the year. He prayed to Magnus that if he sent him fine weather so that he could get back to Orkney he would have him recognized as a saint. The wind died away, and Bishop William sailed safely back to Orkney.

Despite his promise Bishop William did nothing to make Magnus a saint, as he knew that Earl Paul would be angry, as it was his father who had ordered the murder of Magnus. One day while he was praying alone in Christ's Church in Birsay, Bishop William went blind. He stumbled around, but could not even find the door. He prayed to Magnus, saying that if he returned his sight he would make him a saint, whether Earl Paul liked it or not. With that,

his sight returned. Bishop William gathered all the leading men together and told them that he intended to dig up the bones of Magnus. When the grave was opened they found that the coffin had already risen up nearly to the surface. A knuckle bone was placed in fire that had been made holy, but it wouldn't burn. It was said that it took on a golden colour, and even changed into the shape of a cross. After the test they were happy that Magnus should be made a saint, and his bones were placed in a shrine above the altar.

A farmer in Westray called Gunni had a dream one night. In his dream St Magnus came to him and said that he wanted his bones to be removed from Birsay and taken to Kirkwall. If he was taken there he would perform miracles to cure the sick. Gunni woke up scared, he didn't want Earl Paul to know that he was speaking for St Magnus so he stayed at home and said nothing. The next night St Magnus came to him again in his dreams, but this time he was angry. He ordered him to go to Birsay and tell the bishop that he wanted to go east. If he did not do this, then he would suffer in this life and in the next. Gunni went to Birsay and told of his dream in front of the whole congregation after Mass. Many people were there, including Earl Paul. The earl said nothing, but his face flushed red with anger.

Bishop William led a great procession from Birsay to Kirkwall where St Magnus's bones were placed above the high altar of the church that was there. At that time Kirkwall was only a small trading town with few houses and a small church dedicated to St Olaf. Soon the place became well known for the miracles that happened at the shrine of St Magnus.

ᛏᚺᛁ ᛋᚺᛟᚱᛏᛁᚱ ᛟᚱᚲᚺᚹᚨᛁᚾᚷᚨ ᛋᚨᚷᚨ

THE BATTLE OF TANKERNESS

In Norway there was a young man called Kali Kolsson. He was a popular man, strong with light chestnut hair and skilled in games, music, poetry and warfare. His father was called Kol, and his mother was Gunnhild, a sister of St Magnus. He made a claim for half of the earldom of Orkney, which was granted by King Sigurd. The king also gave him a new name. He called him Rognvald, after Earl Rognvald Brusisson who was killed by Earl Thorfinn the Mighty. He said it was because Rognvald was the best of all of the earls of Orkney. Messengers were sent to Earl Paul, asking him to share the earldom. He became very angry and refused. The messengers then went to Sutherland to the evil Frakokk, the woman who had made the poisoned shirt that had killed Earl Harald Smooth-Tongue. Rogvaldur offered to give half of the earldom with her grandson, Olvir Brawl, if she raised an army to support him. She agreed, and said that her army would attack Earl Paul the Silent the following midsummer.

Rognvald chose a band of trusted warriors and sailed from Norway with five or six ships. They landed in Shetland, where they were forced to shelter from a storm. Earl Paul heard that Rognvald was in Shetland and

ᛏᚺᛖ ᛋᚺᛟᚱᛗᛖᚱ ᛟᚱᚲᚾᛁᚪᛁᚾᚷᚪ ᛋᚪᚷᚪ

that Olvir Brawl was going to attack from the south. He decided to sail north to attack Rognvald before Olvir arrived. As his ships began to sail north he was told that longships had been seen sailing across the Pentland Firth, so he turned to attack them. Olvir Brawl had only twelve ships, all small and with few warriors.

The two fleets met off Tankerness and a bloody battle was fought. Earl Paul soon had the best of the battle, as his larger ships cleared the smaller ones. Olvir Brawl's own ship was larger than the rest, and he sailed it at Earl Paul's ship. He attacked, and fought so fiercely that the earl's men were soon driven back. Olvir Brawl sprang onto the earl's ship and threw his spear right at Earl Paul. The spear struck Paul's shield, but the force of it knocked him to the ground. One of Earl Paul's men, a huge warrior called Svein Brest-Rope, picked up a large stone and threw it at Olvir Brawl. The stone hit Olvir on the chest with such force that it knocked him over the side of the ship and into the sea. His men pulled him out of the water, but they didn't know if he was alive or dead. Olvir's ships turned and sailed away. When Olvir came to his senses it was too late to lead another attack, Earl Paul's ships were chasing them back south.

Earl Paul returned to the scene of the battle and captured the ships that Olvir's men had left behind. He then sailed north to Shetland where he captured Rognvald's ships while he and his warriors were ashore. Rognvald and his men challenged him to come ashore and fight, but Paul sailed away with all of the ships. Rognvald had to return to Norway in disgrace, having to sail as a passenger on a cargo ship.

ᛏᚼᛁ ᛋᚼᛟᚱᛏᛘᚱ ᛟᚱᚲᚼᛗᛅᛁᚾᚷᚨ ᛋᚨᚷᚨ

THE KILLING AT ORPHIR

Earl Paul held a great feast in Orphir that Christmas, with many warriors invited as guests. One young man who was there was Svein Asleifsson. His father had been murdered in Caithness by Olvir Brawl and his men, who had set his house on fire. Young Svein had gone to Earl Paul and was given a seat next to the earl. Across the table from him sat the huge warrior Svein Breast-Rope with a relation of his called Jon. When it was late, they all went to their bed. All except Svein Breast-Rope, who sat outside trying to raise the ghosts of the dead. He still believed in the old gods, and was no friend of the church.

The following day the feasting and drinking started again. Svein Breast-Rope had hated Svein Asleifsson's father, and his hatred towards the young man grew as he drank. Breast-Rope complained that his ale horn was being filled up faster than young Svein's one, and that he was not playing fair at the drinking. A warrior named Eyvind handed a larger drinking horn to Svein Asleifsson, who offered it to Breast-Rope. This made Breast-Rope very angry, and he muttered a threat, loud enough for those next to him to hear; 'Svein will kill Svein, and Svein shall kill Svein.'

When the crowd left to go to church Svein Asleifsson was stopped by Eyvind. He told him what Breast-Rope had said, and he gave him an axe and a piece of advice. He said that he must strike first, if he wanted to stay alive. He should hide among the beer barrels that stood next to the door. When Breast-Rope left the building he would be in the company of his relation Jon. If Jon was walking in front of him he should strike Breast-Rope from the front, but if Jon was walking behind him he should strike him from behind. After a short while, Svein Breast-Rope walked over to where Svein Asleifsson was hiding. Jon was walking in front of him. Svein swung his axe and struck Breast-Rope a blow to the forehead. The huge warrior staggered, but did not fall. In the dark doorway he saw the figure of a man, and thought that it was the man who had attacked him, but it was in fact Jon. He swung his sword and split the man's head in two. Jon fell to the floor dead and Breast-Rope fell on top of him. He died soon after.

Svein Asleifsson escaped on horseback over the Orphir Hills and over the Bay of Firth to the island of Damsay. He then travelled to Egilsay, where Bishop William made him welcome. The bishop hated Breast-Rope, as he still worshipped the old gods. When the bodies of the two men were found it was thought that they had killed each other, but when the earl found out that Svein Asleifsson had gone, the blame was put on him. The earl said that he must have had a reason for doing this, but if he didn't come to see him and explain, then it would be worse for him. The winter passed, and there was still no sign of Svein. The earl became angry, and made him an outlaw and took all his family's land in Orkney.

THE VOW

Earl Paul had warning beacons built on Fair Isle, North Ronaldsay, and on the highest hills of most of the other islands. They would be lit if Rognvald tried to invade Orkney again, and the local people would take up their weapons and rush to Earl Paul's defence. The Fair Isle beacon was very important, as Rognvald was on friendly terms with the Shetlanders, but he was not so popular in Orkney. It was likely that an invasion would come from Shetland, and the Fair Isle beacon would be the first warning to Orkney that Rognvald was on his way. A farmer called Dagfinn was put in charge of the Fair Isle beacon. He had to keep a watch for ships, keep the wood of the beacon dry, and light it if there was any sign of danger.

Rognvald's father Kol was now in charge of the invasion of Orkney. He had put together a fleet of ships, raised an army and bought weapons. The fleet sailed to Bergen where Rognvald was given a fully fitted out longship as a gift from his friend, King Harald Gilli, who now ruled all of Norway. While they were waiting for a good wind to sail to Orkney, Kol gave his son a piece of advice. He said that he would have a hard battle in Orkney, as the people would not support him. But if he had the support of the one who had the rightful claim to the islands, his uncle St

Magnus, then he couldn't fail. He told him to make a vow to build a fine stone minster in Kirkwall, finer than any other church in Orkney, and dedicate it to St Magnus. This was agreed, and vows were sworn. The fleet sailed west to Shetland where they were warmly welcomed.

ᛏᚺᛖ ᛋᚺᛟᚱᛏᛖᚱ ᛟᚱᚲᚾᛖᛁᛁᚾᚷᚨ ᛋᚨᚷᚨ

CUNNING PLANS

Rognvald's father Kol asked a cunning old man called Uni for advice on how to deal with the warning beacons. He said that he would deal with it himself, and set off. Kol then had several small ships row to Fair Isle, just far enough so that they could be seen. He then had the sail hoisted half way up the mast, while the oarsmen rowed backwards so that the ships didn't move much. He then ordered the sail to be hoisted higher so it looked like they were getting nearer. When this was seen from Fair Isle Dagfinn lit the warning beacon. The fire was seen in North Ronaldsay where a man called Thorstein lit the beacon that was there. Soon all of the warning beacons were ablaze, and the people were rushing to Earl Paul's defence with swords and spears. Kol ordered his ships back to Shetland.

When all the chiefs were gathered together around Earl Paul nobody knew what was going on. There was no sign of the invasion and people were starting to argue. Dagfinn was blamed for lighting the Fair Isle beacon, but he turned around and blamed Thorstein of North Ronaldsay for lighting his beacon first. Thorstein said that he had lit his beacon because the Fair Isle beacon was alight. The argument got worse, and Thorstein drew out his axe and killed Dagfinn. The warriors started to fight with each

ᛏᚺᛉ ᛏᚺᛟᚱᛒᛖᚱ ᛟᚱᚲᚺᛉᛁᚾᚷᛖ ᛋᚨᚷᚨ

other, but were ordered to stop by Earl Paul.

Uni and three young men rowed a small fishing boat to Fair Isle. He claimed that the boys were his sons and that they had been robbed by Rognvald's men. They were taken in and treated kindly. The boys went back to their fishing, while the old man stayed behind. He soon made friends with the local people, who had no idea that he was working for Rognvald.

There was a man called Eirik who was now in charge of the warning beacon. Old Uni offered to look after the beacon for him, as he said he was sitting around doing nothing all day. Eirik was pleased with the offer and Uni sat by the beacon. When there was nobody around Uni carried buckets of water to the beacon and soaked all of the wood so that it wouldn't burn. At the same time the sails of Rognvald's invasion fleet were seen. People ran to light the beacon, but found old Uni had gone and the beacon was too wet to burn. Rognvald's ships sailed to Westray and captured the island. Messengers were sent to Bishop William, asking him to speak to Earl Paul. He got Earl Paul's word that there would be a two-week truce between the two sides while they decided what to do next.

ᛏᚼᛉ ᛋᚼᚨᚱᛏᛉᚱ ᚨᚱᚲᚼᛏᚨᛁᚾᚷᚨ ᛋᚨᚷᚨ

KIDNAPPED

Svein Asleifsson had been in hiding in the Hebrides. He left there and went to see Earl Maddad in Athol, who was married to Earl Paul's sister Margaret. They talked a lot about the possibility of their son Harald sharing part of the earldom of Orkney. While he was in Athol Svein heard of Rognvald's invasion of Orkney, and he returned home with thirty men in a cargo ship. Earl Paul was staying with his friend Sigurd at Westness in Rousay. Paul had gone to hunt otters among the rocks with a group of his warriors. Svein was passing in his ship when he saw the men on Rousay, and ordered twenty of his men to hide in the bottom of the ship while they went to see who it was. They spoke to the warriors and found out that the earl was with them. They rowed out of sight, and then they went ashore and attacked. Earl Paul's men were killed and the earl was carried away by Svein. They sailed south to Athol where Earl Paul was held prisoner by his sister Margaret and her husband, Earl Maddad. It was said that Margaret paid Svein to blind Earl Paul, and cast him into a dungeon. She later hired a man to kill him, so that her son Harald should have his half share of Orkney.

ᛏᚺᛁ ᛊᚺᛟᚱᛏᛖᚱ ᛟᚱᚲᚲᛘᚨᛁᚾᚷᚨ ᛊᚨᚷᚨ

ROGNVALD BECOMES EARL

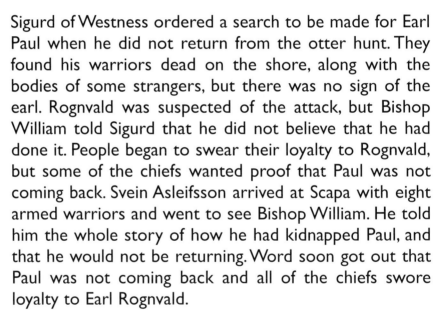

Sigurd of Westness ordered a search to be made for Earl Paul when he did not return from the otter hunt. They found his warriors dead on the shore, along with the bodies of some strangers, but there was no sign of the earl. Rognvald was suspected of the attack, but Bishop William told Sigurd that he did not believe that he had done it. People began to swear their loyalty to Rognvald, but some of the chiefs wanted proof that Paul was not coming back. Svein Asleifsson arrived at Scapa with eight armed warriors and went to see Bishop William. He told him the whole story of how he had kidnapped Paul, and that he would not be returning. Word soon got out that Paul was not coming back and all of the chiefs swore loyalty to Earl Rognvald.

Rognvald ordered work to start on building the cathedral in honour of his uncle St Magnus. His father, Kol, took charge of the building work, and soon the walls of the building started to rise. After a while the money ran out, so Earl Rognvald offered the people of Orkney the right to buy back their land that Earl Turf Einar had taken from them. The people agreed, and soon there was enough money to finish the great cathedral in Kirkwall.

ᛏᚼᛉ ᛊᚼᛟᚱᛏᛉᚱ ᛟᚱᚲᚻᚤᛆᛁᚾᚷᚨ ᛊᚨᚷᚨ

After two years Earl Rognvald was visited by Bishop Jon of Athol, who asked for half of the earldom for Earl Maddad's son Harald. The claim was a good one, and Rognvald agreed to share the islands. The boy was taken to Orkney where he was fostered by Thorbjorn Clerk, the grandson of the evil Frakokk. Svein Asleifsson later attacked Frakokk's house in Sutherland in revenge for Olvir Brawl killing his father. Frakokk was killed, and Olvir ran away to the Hebrides and was never heard of again.

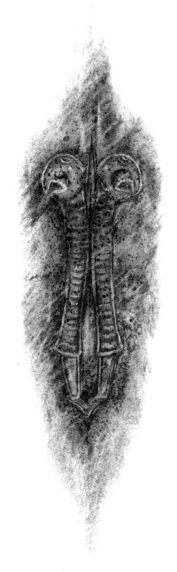

ᛏᚼᛁ ᛖᚼᚫᚱᛏᚢᚱ ᚫᚱᚲᛁᚤᛗᚫᛁᚼᚷᚫ ᛖᚠᛁᚴᚠ

THE PILGRIMAGE

Earl Rognvald was invited to Norway to see King Ingi, the son of his friend King Harald. He brought Earl Harald Maddadsson with him, who was a youth at the time. When they were there a warrior called Eindridi the Young arrived back from Constantinople. He was full of stories of the Holy Land and the battles that he had fought in, and Earl Rognvald spent a long time talking to him about his adventures. Eindridi told Earl Rognvald that he should make a pilgrimage to the Holy Land, as it would add to his honour. Other people said that if he led them, then they would follow him. Rognvald decided to make the journey after two years, and it was agreed that no man would have a ship with more than thirty oars, and that no ship should be decorated with paint or gold. This was to stop the chieftains from getting jealous of each other.

When the time came, Rognvald left Orkney and sailed to Norway, where a ship had been built for him. It was a beautiful ship with thirty five rowing benches, and decorated with gold at the prow and stern. Eindridi, who was to be their guide, delayed them as he kept saying that his ship was not ready. When they finally sailed west back to Orkney, Earl Rognvald led the way in his fine new ship. Suddenly two ships sailed up and went past them. It was Eindridi in a huge ship with a dragon's head at its prow

ᛏᚼᛁ ᛋᚼᛟᚱᛏᛖᚱ ᛟᚱᚲᚾᛃᛅᛁᚾᚷᚨ ᛋᛅᚷᚨ

and decorated all over with gold and brightly coloured paint. He had ignored the earl's command about the size of ships and their decoration. The fleet arrived in Orkney, but there was no sign of Eindridi and his fine dragon ship. They were intending to stay in Orkney for the winter and leave in the spring. After a while they finally heard that Eindridi's fine new dragon ship had been wrecked off of Shetland and that he was having a new ship built in Norway. Yet again Eindridi had delayed the pilgrimage.

ᛏᚺᛖ ᛖᛁᚾᛞᚱᛁᛞᛁᚱ ᛟᚱᚲᚺᛋᛅᛁᚾᚷᚨ ᛋᚨᚷᚨ

QUEEN ERMINGERD

Earl Rognvald left the earldom in Earl Harald's hands and sailed south to England. He had Bishop William with him, as he was a wise man and could speak many languages. They then sailed to France, stopping at Narbonne where they were treated well. The earl there had died, leaving his young and beautiful daughter Ermingerd as Queen. She gave feasts in honour of Earl Rognvald and the most important men who sailed with him. They were all very taken with Ermingerd's beauty, and Earl Rognvald made many poems in her honour. It was obvious that Rognvald and Ermingerd liked each other, and the local noblemen were keen for him to

marry her and to settle there as king. Rognvald said that he wanted to carry on his journey, but he said that he would call in to see her on his return from the Holy Land.

ᛏᚼᛉ ᛊᚼᛟᚱᛏᛗᚱ ᛟᚱᚲᚾᚢᛆᛁᚾᚷᚠ ᛊᚠᚷᚠ

THE CASTLE

Earl Rognvald and his men sailed to Galicia in Spain, where they tried to buy supplies from the local traders. They were told that the people had little to sell, as a band of warriors had arrived from another country and were living in a nearby castle. They raided and carried off whatever they wanted, so that the people had little food left to sell. They made Earl Rognvald an offer, that if he and his warriors would fight these men and capture the castle then they would sell them what food they had. They also said that whatever treasure they found in the castle was theirs to keep. Rognvald agreed, and asked a wise man called Erling Wry-Neck what was the best way of capturing the castle. Erling said that the mortar that held the stones together looked weak, and if they set a fire against it, it would crumble and the walls would fall down. Rognvald ordered his men to cut down trees to pile against the castle walls. Before they could carry out their plan Bishop William stopped them, as it was Christmas and not a time for war. They waited until Christmas was over before they attacked.

The chieftain inside the castle was called Godfrey, a cunning and evil man. He had travelled over many lands, and knew many languages. He dressed in rags like a beggar, and then had himself lowered over the castle walls

on a rope. He went around Earl Rognvald's camp begging for scraps of food, but what he was really doing was listening to what his enemies were planning to do. He saw that the Norsemen were split into two camps, those who followed Earl Rognvald and those who followed Eindridi the Young. He spoke with Eindridi, and he soon saw that he was a greedy and selfish man who could be easily bought. He said that his master had sent him to ask for help to escape from the castle, and offered Eindridi a great treasure if he would help him. Eindridi was keen to have the money, even if it meant betraying his comrades.

After Christmas Earl Rognvald had the war trumpets sounded and the wood was piled up around the rampart walls that surrounded the castle. As Erling had predicted, the walls crumbled and fell, and Rognvald's men attacked. Burning sulphur and pitch was poured from the castle walls, but it did little damage. The Norsemen stormed the castle, and a fierce fight began. Many of the castle's defenders were killed in the battle. Thick smoke blew over the battlefield, right over where Eindridi and his followers were standing. Godfrey ran from the castle, and Eindridi helped him to escape into the nearby woods. The castle was looted, but there was no sign of Godfrey. Eindridi was suspected of having let him go, but it couldn't be proved. The fleet then sailed through the Straits of Gibraltar and into the Mediterranean Sea. Here Eindridi's ship and six others left the Earl's fleet and sailed north to France. This was proof that Eindridi was a traitor who had sold himself to Godfrey.

THE BATTLE WITH THE DROMOND

As the fleet sailed through the Mediterranean they thought they saw two islands, but later when the fog had cleared they could only see one. They thought that the other island must have been a dromond, one of the huge ships that traders in the area used. Rognvald called a meeting and asked his men how they should attack this ship, as it was such a huge size. Erling Wry-Neck said that it was so big that if their ships pulled in close to it, anything thrown from the ship would miss them as they would be sheltered by its overhanging sides. It was agreed that they should attack, and the fleet set off after the dromond.

When they caught up with the great ship the Saracens onboard it took out their rich goods, and they laughed at Earl Rognvald's men. They thought that there was no way that their huge ship could be captured. The Norsemen steered their ships in under the side of the ship, three on each side, but it was so big that their swords couldn't reach the deck. The Saracens poured sulphur and boiling pitch over the side of their ship, but it mostly missed the Earl's ships because they were sheltered under the great ship's sides. Bishop William ordered his ship to steer away

from the dromond, and along with another ship they attacked it with arrows. The Saracens were so busy protecting themselves from the arrows that they didn't notice Earl Rognvald take his axe and start to cut his way through the side of the ship. Others did the same, and soon they were through the side of the ship and they got onboard. They attacked the Saracens and soon had killed them all.

They looted the ship of all of its goods, and captured a huge man who looked like he was wealthy. After that they set the dromond on fire. The captured man refused to speak, but he sat and stared at the burning dromond. Soon it looked as if rivers of gold were pouring out of its sides. The wealthy Saracen was a nobleman, and he was carrying a large amount of gold and silver, which had been hidden on the ship. Rognvald's men had not found it, and it was now melting in the heat of the fire. Rognvald put the man ashore in Africa, but as they had spared his life he didn't have them attacked by his own men.

THE SHORTER ORKNEYINGA SAGA

THE RETURN HOME

Earl Rognvald's fleet sailed to the island of Crete, then on to the Holy Land. Rognvald bathed in the River Jordan, and spent some time in that country. As the year grew older they sailed for the great city of Constantinople, where they were warmly welcomed by the emperor. He gave them rich presents, and offered to hire them as members of the Varangian Guard, his own personal bodyguards. It was here that they found Eindridi the Young with his followers. He tried to cause trouble for them whenever he could and tried to spread false stories about them. Years later Erling Wry-Neck would become the King of Norway and Eindridi the Young would fight against him in support of King Hakon the Broad-Shouldered. In the end Hakon was killed and King Erling captured Eindridi and had him executed at Oslo.

Rognvald left Constantinople that winter and sailed to Durazzo in Bulgaria, and then on to Puglia in Italy where they took horses and rode to Rome. They then took the pilgrim route north, riding to Denmark then back to Norway. They were given a heroes welcome when they returned, and it was said that their journey added greatly to their fame.

ᛏᚺᛖ ᛋᚺᛟᚱᛗᛖᚱ ᛟᚱᚲᚺᛗᚨᛁᚾᚷᚨ ᛋᚨᚷᚨ

EARL ERLEND MAKES WAR

On his return to Norway Earl Rognvald was told that there was war raging in Orkney. On one side was Earl Harald Maddadsson, while on the other was Svein Asleifsson and Erlend Haraldsson. Erlend was the son of Earl Harald Smooth-Tongue, who had died after putting on the poisoned shirt. He had been granted half of Caithness by the King of Scots and now wanted half of Orkney too. Earl Harald had fallen out with Svein Asleifsson, who had decided to back Erlend in revenge. Erlend had gone to Norway and was granted Harald's half of Orkney. Svein told him that he must act quickly, before Harald found out what the king had decided. They sailed to Cairston in Stromness where Harald's fleet was anchored, and attacked him. Harald and his men ran into the fortress that stood there ready for the attack. One man called Arni Ravensson was so scared that he ran all the way from Cairston to Kirkwall. He got stuck in the cathedral door when he tried to run into it with his shield still slung over his back, as he was so frightened that he had forgotten that it was there. The two earls fought a long and hard battle, which only ended when it grew dark. The local farmers went between the two earls and tried to make peace, but Erlend was not interested. It ended up

ᛏᚼᛁ ᛋᚼᚭᚱᛏᛁᚱ ᚭᚱᚲᚾᚢᛅᛁᚾᚷᚭ ᛋᚭᚷᚭ

that Harald had to give up his half of Orkney and swear to leave and to never return.

ᛏᚺᛖ ᛊᚺᛟᚱᛏᛖᚱ ᛟᚱᚲᚾᛖᛁᛜᚨ ᛊᚨᚷᚨ

THE WAR OF THE THREE EARLS

Earl Rognvald returned to Orkney and all the people were glad to see him. Messengers from Earl Erlend went to see him and offered a peace meeting. Rognvald met Erlend, and they swore an oath to rule Orkney together and to defend the islands from Harald.

Some time later Earl Rognvald was in Caithness celebrating his daughter's wedding, when messengers from Harald asked him for a meeting. Rognvald met Harald and they agreed to share the earldom and to attack Erlend. They sailed to Orkney, forcing Erlend and Svein Asleifsson to run. After Erlend and Svein had spent some time raiding in Caithness they returned to Orkney and took the two earls by surprise. Erlend had heard that Harald's ships were anchored at Scapa, and sailed his ships in for the attack. The first that Harald knew of the attack was when the war horn was sounded and the warriors were on them. A hard and bloody battle was fought, but Erlend's men won a great victory, capturing Harald's ships and forcing him to run for his life. Erlend's men were then told that Rognvald was staying with a farmer at Knarston, and they set off to capture him. They

ᛏᚺᛁ ᛋᚺᛟᚱᛏᛁᚱ ᛟᚱᚲᚺᚤᛗᛁᚾᚷᚨ ᛋᚨᚷᚨ

were met by the farmer, called Botolf the Stubborn, who told them that Earl Rognvald had gone to shoot grouse on the moors with his friends. After they had run off to catch the earl, Botolf went to Rognvald and woke him up, telling him of the danger. Rognvald returned to his hall at Orphir where he found Harald in hiding. They both took ships and sailed to Caithness.

Svein warned Erlend to take his ships to South Walls, where he could watch the Pentland Firth in case the two earls returned. It was coming up for Christmas and Erlend's men argued that they should go to the small island of Damsay where there was a great hall. Erlend agreed, but Svein warned him to sleep in his ship and not ashore. Erlend and his men ignored Svein's advice, and slept in the warmth and comfort of the great hall. Svein heard of this and sent a messenger to warn Erlend that he was still in danger, and to sleep in his ship. Erlend agreed, but many of his men did not take the warning seriously and remained ashore.

Suddenly, without any warning, Earl Rognvald and Earl Harald attacked the ship with many warriors. Erlend was drunk, and had to be carried away by a loyal warrior. The two earls soon killed many of Erlend's men and captured the rest. There was no sign of Erlend until two days before Christmas, when a spear was seen sticking out of a pile of seaweed. When people pulled the seaweed away they found the body of Earl Erlend, which had the spear driven through it. His followers were spared and they swore loyalty to the two earls, while others took sanctuary in St Magnus Cathedral until they were pardoned. The body of Earl Erlend was carried to Kirkwall and buried in the wall of the cathedral.

ᛏᚺᛖ ᛊᚺᛟᚱᛏᛖᚱ ᛟᚱᚲᚾᛁᛁᚾᚷᚨ ᛊᚨᚷᚨ

THE MURDER OF EARL ROGNVALD

Svein Asleifsson had been on the run since the death of Earl Erlend, but Earl Rognvald was keen to have him as a friend. After much fighting and bitterness, Svein and Earl Harald became friends again. Earl Harald's foster-father, Thorbjorn Clerk, had fallen out with Earl Rognvald and had been driven out of Orkney. He lived in Caithness, where he murdered and stole as he pleased.

In the summer of 1158 Earl Rognvald and Earl Harald went to Caithness to hunt red deer. Rognvald heard a rumour that Thorbjorn Clerk was in the area and set off with twenty horsemen and a hundred foot soldiers. They arrived at a farm owned by a man called Hallvard, who was a good friend of Thorbjorn. He was building a haystack, and shouted out Rognvald's name when he rode up, pretending that it was a greeting. Thorbjorn Clerk was in the house and when he heard Hallvard shout Rognvald's name he ran out with his warriors to attack. There was a path that led to the house that was so narrow and deep that only one rider at a time could use it. Thorbjorn swung his sword at Rognvald, but a young man called Asolf put out his arm to protect the earl and had his right hand cut off. Rognvald was wounded on the

chin. He tried to get off his horse, but his foot got stuck in the stirrup and he was run through with a spear. Thorbjorn and his men ran off when Earl Harald and his warriors arrived. They found Earl Rognvald dying, and Harald was forced to chase Thorbjorn. Earl Harald was in a difficult position, as Thorbjorn had been his foster-father. Thorbjorn and his men were attacked, but Thorbjorn begged Harald to let him go. Harald could not spare him, as it would look like he was involved in the murder. Thorbjorn and his men ran to hide in a small house, but it was set on fire and they were forced to come out and were killed.

The body of Earl Rognvald was carried back to Orkney and buried in the cathedral that he had built in honour of his uncle St Magnus. It is said that miracles took place at Rognvald's tomb. Some time later Bishop Bjarni Kolbeinsson had him made a saint.

ᛏᚼᛁ ᛋᚼᛟᚱᛏᛖᚱ ᛟᚱᚲᚤᛗᛅᛁᚾᚷᛅ ᛋᚨᚷᚨ

THE KILLING OF SVEIN

Svein Asleifsson lived on the island of Gairsay where he had the largest drinking hall in all of Orkney. He had a large number of warriors living with him and he was very rich and powerful. He went on two viking raids every year. After the seeds had been sown he went on his 'spring-trip,' returning to gather in the harvest before going on his 'autumn-trip.' One spring he was raiding in the Hebrides and in Ireland when he captured two English cargo ships. They were full of riches, including beautiful cloth. Svein ordered the cloth to be sewn onto the sails of his longships so that they made a great show when they arrived home in Gairsay.

After his return he invited Earl Harald to come to a feast. The earl asked Svein to give up raiding, as he was getting too old for such a dangerous lifestyle. Svein agreed, but said that he wanted to go on just one last raid that autumn to see if he could capture as much riches as he had done in spring. The earl agreed, and Svein planned his last viking raid.

That autumn Svein set off with seven large longships and went to Ireland where he attacked Dublin. The town

ᛏᚺᛁ ᛋᚺᛟᚱᛏᛁᚱ ᛟᚱᚲᚾᛁᚨᛁᚾᚷᚨ ᛋᚨᚷᚨ

surrendered to Svein and the townspeople agreed that Svein would put his own men in charge and that the town would pay taxes to them. They agreed to go back to their ships and to return the next morning. That night the people of Dublin dug deep pits in front of the town gates and between the houses. They covered them over with thin branches and put straw on top to hide them. The next morning Svein arrived with his warriors and was met by the townspeople who stood on either side of the pits. Svein suspected nothing, and walked with his men towards the pits. They fell through the thin covering and were trapped. The town gates were closed and barred and the warriors were attacked. They could not defend themselves and were all killed. It was said that Svein was the last one to die. His last words were, 'Whether or not I am to fall today, I want everyone to know that I'm the retainer of the holy Earl Rognvald, and now he's with God, it's in him I'll put my trust.'

ᛏᚺᛁ ᛇᚺᛜᚱᛏᛖᚱ ᛜᚱᚲᚺᚹᚨᛁᚾᚷᚨ ᛇᚨᚷᚨ

HARALD THE YOUNG

Earl Rognvald's oldest grandson was called Harald the Young. He went to see King William of Scotland and asked him for half of the Earldom of Caithness, which the king gave him. He then sent messengers to Earl Harald, who was now known as Harald the Old, and asked for the half share of Orkney. Harald the Old said that he would never share the earldom. Harald the Young sent a spy to Orkney to see what Earl Harald the Old was doing. Harald the Old had been gathering a huge fleet of ships in South Ronaldsay ready to attack Harald the Young in Caithness. He was advised to go to Thurso to try to raise men, but he stayed where he was and prepared to fight.

Earl Harald the Old's fleet arrived, and a huge number of warriors attacked Harald

the Young's men. They were hopelessly outnumbered, but put up a brave fight. Harald the Young was killed on a piece of moorland used for cutting peats. It was said that a great light was seen over the spot where he was killed and that a church was later built there. Many miracles were performed at his grave and he was regarded as a saint.

ᛏᚼᛉ ᛖᚼᛟᚱᛏᛉᚱ ᛟᚱᚲᚲᚿᛅᛁᚾᚷᚨ ᛖᚨᚷᚨ

THE LOSS OF SHETLAND

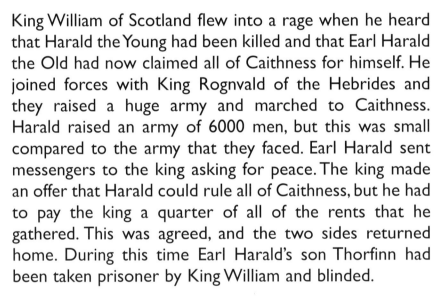

King William of Scotland flew into a rage when he heard that Harald the Young had been killed and that Earl Harald the Old had now claimed all of Caithness for himself. He joined forces with King Rognvald of the Hebrides and they raised a huge army and marched to Caithness. Harald raised an army of 6000 men, but this was small compared to the army that they faced. Earl Harald sent messengers to the king asking for peace. The king made an offer that Harald could rule all of Caithness, but he had to pay the king a quarter of all of the rents that he gathered. This was agreed, and the two sides returned home. During this time Earl Harald's son Thorfinn had been taken prisoner by King William and blinded.

Harald was soon in trouble again, as his brother-in-law had raised an army in Orkney to fight in a civil war between rival kings in Norway. Many of the Orcadians and the king that they supported were killed, and King Sverrir now wanted his revenge. He blamed Earl Harald for supporting his rival, and ordered him to come to Norway. Harald brought Bishop Bjarni Kolbeinsson with him to plead his case. King Sverrir told Earl Harald that he was taking back all of Shetland from him, along with all the